OWJC

11/11

COMMUNITY · CONNECTIONS

HOW DOES IT FLY?
BOMBER PLANE

BY MATT MULLINS

Published in the United States of America by Cherry Lake Publishing
Ann Arbor, Michigan
www.cherrylakepublishing.com

Content Adviser: Jacob Zeiger, Production Support Engineer, the Boeing Company

Photo Credits: Cover and page 1, ©Elvele Images Ltd/Alamy;
page 5, ©Mark Beton/England/Alamy; page 7, ©Peter Brogden/Alamy;
page 9, ©Russell Shively/Shutterstock, Inc.; page 11, ©Peter Steiner/Alamy;
page 13, ©david pearson/Alamy; page 15, ©Laurin Rinder/Dreamstime.com;
page 17, ©Peter Baxter/Shutterstock, Inc.; page 19, ©Dan Lee/Shutterstock, Inc.;
page 21, ©George Bailey/Dreamstime.com.

LIBRARY OF CONGRESS CATALOGING-IN-PUBLICATION DATA
Mullins, Matt.
  How does it fly? Bomber plane/by Matt Mullins.
    p. cm.—(Community connections)
  Includes bibliographical references and index.
  ISBN-13: 978-1-61080-067-9 (library binding)
  ISBN-10: 1-61080-067-2 (library binding)
  1. Bombers—Juvenile literature. I. Title. II. Title: Bomber plane.
III. Title. IV. Series.
  UG1242.B6M84 2011
  623.74'63—dc22   2010051583

Cherry Lake Publishing would like to acknowledge the
work of The Partnership for 21st Century Skills. Please
visit www.21stcenturyskills.org for more information.

Printed in the United States of America
Corporate Graphics Inc.
July 2011
CLFA09

BOMBER PLANE

CONTENTS

HOW DOES IT FLY?

MAJOR MILITARY PLANES

You do not see bomber planes very often. If you are lucky, you may see one at a military air base. You have probably seen them in pictures, though. Maybe they were flying. Maybe you saw some in a movie.

Visitors flock to take a look at a Vulcan bomber.

Bomber planes are often very large. One of the most used bombers is the B-52. Its **wingspan** stretches more than half the length of a football field.

Other planes, such as **fighters**, are usually much smaller. An F-16 fighter could fit under a B-52's wing, with room to spare!

The B-52 bomber has eight engines, four on each wing.

Bombers were important during World War II. Many countries developed new ways of using bombers in battle. What were some of the ways they were used? Ask your teacher, librarian, or parent for help in finding the answers.

7

WHY SO BIG?

Why are bombers so big? Because they carry bombs, and bombs are very heavy.

Bombers usually carry more than one bomb at a time. They also carry bombs over long distances. It takes a big plane to carry these bombs.

Bombers might carry several smaller bombs. Sometimes they carry a few very large bombs.

Planes fly by using **thrust** from engines and **lift** from wings. Engines push the planes forward through the air. Wings keep them up in the air.

Bigger, more powerful engines provide more thrust. Larger wings provide more lift. Bombers usually have long wings and several engines.

The powerful engines of the B-1 bomber drive it forward in flight.

Bombs are kept in the bomb bay. This room has special doors in the floor. These doors open to drop the bombs.

The crew waits until the bomber is over the area to be bombed. Then the crew opens the bay doors and releases the bombs. The bombs explode when they hit the ground.

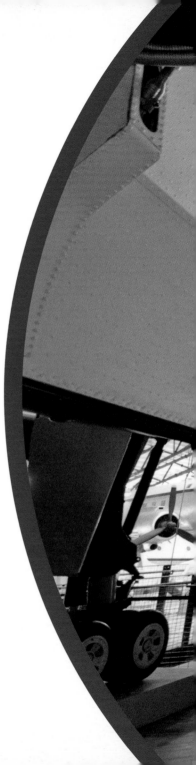

Bomb bay doors are located at the bottom of the bomber. This plane's bomb bay doors are open.

13

EARLY BOMBERS

One of the first bombers was a small fighter biplane. Biplanes have two sets of wings. In 1912, a Bulgarian pilot reached out from the seat of his biplane during a battle. He dropped two **hand grenades** to the ground!

Bombs improved quickly. Several countries developed new bombs that planes could drop.

Early bombers often dove low to the ground for better aim.

Bombers in World War II were usually not fighter planes. The bombers were bigger than the ones used during World War I.

Big bombers were not as quick as fighters. They had guns to protect themselves from other planes. But fighter planes flew alongside bombers to add more protection.

The fighter planes that fly with bombers are called escorts.

CREATE!

Because bombers
are big, they are the
best, right? Not so
fast! Create a list of
what bombers do
best. Make another
list for fighters. Which
abilities are more
important in war?

17

MODERN BOMBERS

Today, there are many bombers of all sizes. The biggest are called heavy bombers. They travel thousands of miles. Their size makes them heavy and slow.

Medium bombers weigh less. They fly shorter distances. Because they are lighter, they can travel at higher speeds.

The B-1 bomber's wings can move. They swing back so the bomber can fly fast and lower to the ground.

19

Some amazing bombers are **stealth** bombers. They hide from enemy **radar**. Enemies cannot spot these planes' locations. Stealth bombers are made with special materials. Some, such as the B-2, have no tail sections. This makes it harder for radar to spot them.

Bombers change as computers and weapons improve. What will they look like tomorrow?

The B-2 bomber is sometimes called the Flying Wing.

Many militaries rely on missiles. Missiles can fly more than 1,000 miles by themselves. Missiles can also be very powerful. How do you think bombers will be affected by technologies such as missiles?

21

GLOSSARY

fighters (FYE-turz) planes used to attack or protect a territory or another aircraft

hand grenades (HAND gruh-NAYDZ) small, handheld containers of explosives

lift (LIFT) the upward force of flight

missiles (MISS-uhlz) weapons that are fired or thrown toward a target

radar (RAY-dar) equipment that uses radio waves to determine the location and movement of objects

stealth (STELTH) technology that makes a plane or other object almost invisible to radar

thrust (THRUHST) the forward force of flight

wingspan (WEENG-span) the distance from the tip of one wing to the tip of its opposite wing

FIND OUT MORE

BOOKS

David, Jack. *B-52 Stratofortresses*. Minneapolis: Bellwether Media, 2009.

Eason, Sarah. *How Does a Jet Plane Work?* New York: Gareth Stevens Publishing, 2010.

Goldish, Meish. *Freaky-Big Airplanes*. New York: Bearport Publishing, 2010.

WEB SITES

Airplanes for Kids
www.airplanesforkids.com/page/page/1292990.htm
Information, pictures, links, jokes, and more about military planes.

NASA Ultra-Efficient Engine Technology: Kid's Page
www.ueet.nasa.gov/StudentSite/
Learn more about how planes fly and the history of flight.

INDEX

ABOUT THE AUTHOR

Matt Mullins lives near an airport in Madison, Wisconsin. Matt has a master's degree in the history of science and writes about all sorts of things—science, technology, business, academics, food, and more. He also writes and directs films and spends time with his son.